UNCOVER
&DISCOVER

What Has a **Harness** and Screeches?
¿Qué tiene un **arnés** y derrapa?

WRITTEN BY **Judy Zocchi**

ILLUSTRATED BY **Russ Daff**

First Printing

Published by dingles&company
P.O. Box 508
Sea Girt, New Jersey 08750

**LIBRARY OF CONGRESS
CATALOG CARD NUMBER**
2007903715

ISBN
978-1-59646-814-6

Printed in the United States
of America

The Uncover & Discover series is
based on the original concept
of Judy Mazzeo Zocchi.

ART DIRECTION & DESIGN
Rizco Design

EDITORIAL CONSULTANT
Andrea Curley

SPANISH EDITOR
Jerina Page

PROJECT MANAGER
Lisa Aldorasi

EDUCATIONAL CONSULTANTS
Melissa Oster and Margaret Bergin

RESEARCH AND ADDITIONAL COPY BY
Robert Kanner

PRE-PRESS
Pixel Graphics

WEBSITE
www.dingles.com

E-MAIL
info@dingles.com

The **Uncover & Discover** series encourages children to inquire, investigate, and use their imagination in an interactive and entertaining manner. This series helps to sharpen their powers of observation, improve reading and writing skills, and apply knowledge across the curriculum.

La serie **Observa y Descubre** motiva a niños y niñas a preguntar, investigar y usar su imaginación de manera interactiva y divertida. La serie ayuda a perfeccionar su capacidad de observación, a mejorar sus habilidades de lecto-escritura, así como a aplicar el conocimiento previo en las diferentes materias del currículo.

Uncover each clue
see what vehicle
when you're done!

una por una, ¡y
que puedes

one by one and

you can **discover**

Observa las pistas,

ve el vehículo

descubrir al final!

I have four specially made rubber **tires**. When I go fast, the rubber softens and gets sticky, which gives me traction.

WHERE IS THE **TIRE**?

¿DÓNDE ESTÁ LA **LLANTA**?

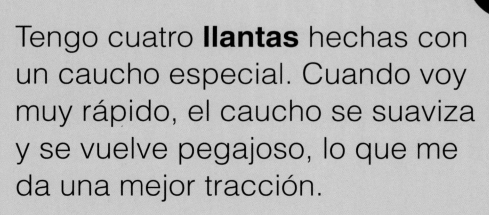

Tengo cuatro **llantas** hechas con un caucho especial. Cuando voy muy rápido, el caucho se suaviza y se vuelve pegajoso, lo que me da una mejor tracción.

I have a **steering wheel** that
can be removed so the driver can
climb into and out of me easily.

LOOK FOR THE **STEERING WHEEL**.

BUSCA EL **VOLANTE**.

Tengo un **volante** que
se puede quitar, para
que el piloto pueda
subir y bajar fácilmente.

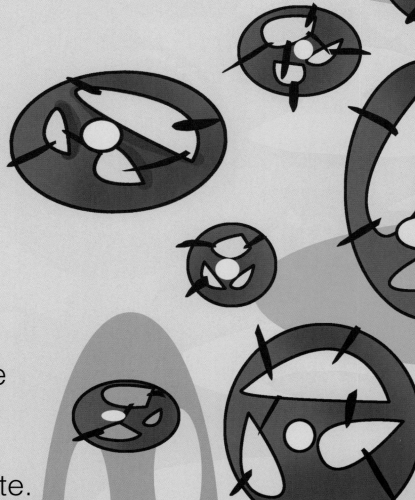

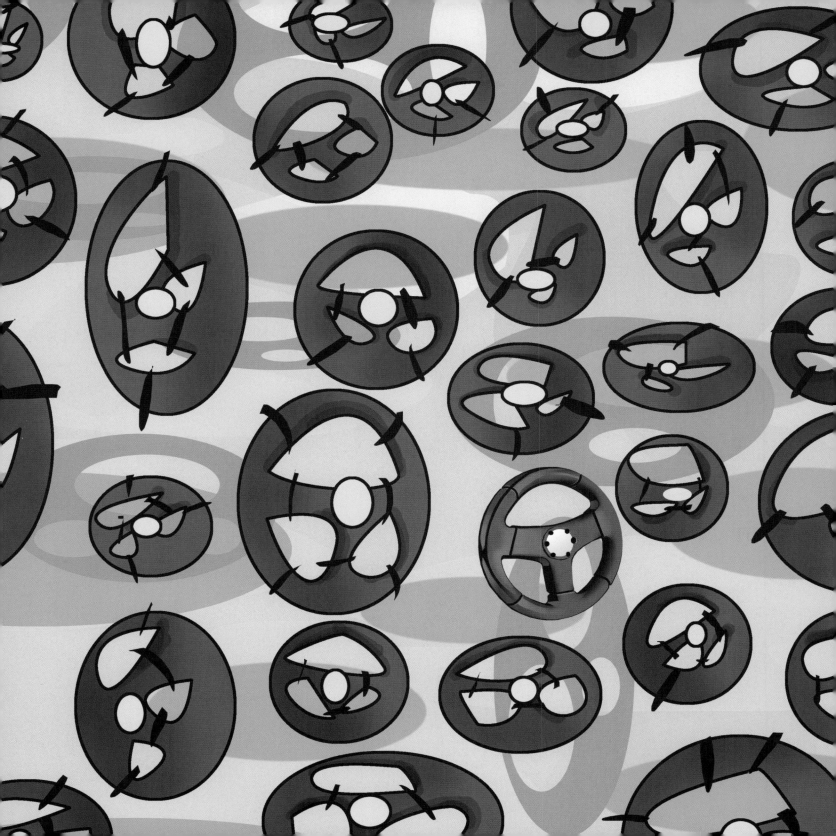

I have stickers of **headlights** instead of real ones so the lights won't shatter and become road hazards.

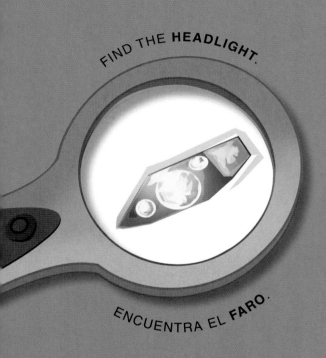

FIND THE **HEADLIGHT**.

ENCUENTRA EL **FARO**.

En lugar de **faros** tengo calcomanías, para que los vidrios no se hagan añicos y sean un peligro en el camino.

My **engine** can produce enough power to keep me going very fast for a long time.

DO YOU SEE THE **ENGINE?**

¿VES EL **MOTOR**?

Mi **motor** produce suficiente poder para ir veloz durante mucho tiempo.

The **number** on my door
identifies me from my competitors.

WHERE IS THE **NUMBER?**

7

¿DÓNDE ESTÁ EL **NÚMERO?**

El **número** de mi puerta
me identifica entre todos
los competidores.

My crew has an **air gun** to quickly remove and tighten the lug nuts that keep my tires in place.

LOOK FOR THE **AIR GUN**.

BUSCA LA **PISTOLA DE AIRE**.

Mi equipo tiene una **pistola de aire** para quitar y apretar las tuercas que mantienen mis llantas en su lugar.

When I need fuel,
my crew uses a **fuel can**
to fill my 22-gallon tank.

FIND THE **FUEL CAN**.

ENCUENTRA EL
DEPÓSITO DE COMBUSTIBLE.

Cuando necesito combustible,
mi equipo utiliza un **depósito
de combustible** para llenar mi
tanque de más de 83 litros.

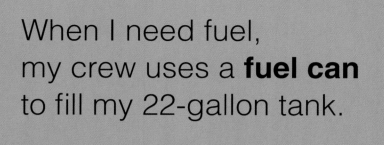

I have a **harness** with straps
to hold my driver in my seat.

DO YOU SEE THE **HARNESS**?

¿VES EL **ARNÉS**?

Tengo un **arnés** de seguridad
con correas para mantener
a mi piloto en el asiento.

My driver wears a **helmet**
to protect his or her head.

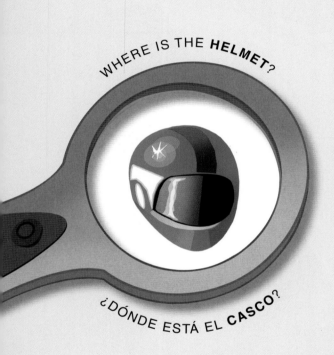

WHERE IS THE **HELMET?**

¿DÓNDE ESTÁ EL **CASCO?**

Mi piloto usa un **casco**
para protegerse la cabeza.

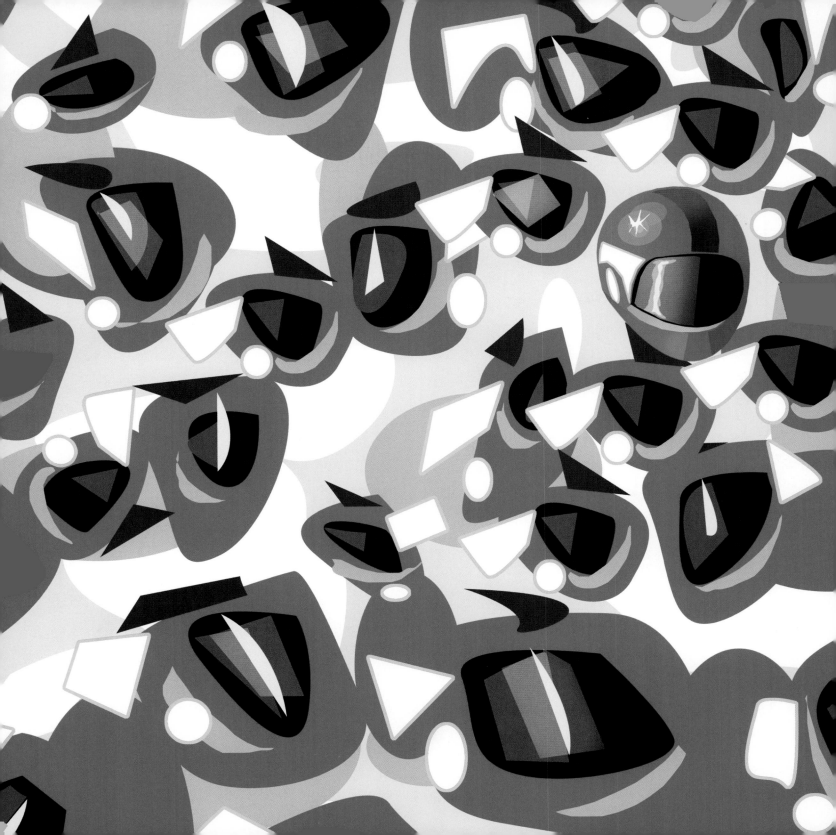

My driver wears a special type of **suit** to protect him or her from getting burned in case of a fire.

LOOK FOR THE **SUIT**.

BUSCA EL **TRAJE**.

Mi piloto usa un **traje** especial que lo protege e impide que se queme en caso de incendio.

I compete on a
track or speedway.

FIND THE **TRACK**.

ENCUENTRA LA **PISTA**.

Compito en una
pista o en un circuito.

My driver knows the race is over when the black-and-white checkered **flag** is waved.

DO YOU SEE THE **FLAG**?

¿VES LA **BANDERA**?

Mi piloto sabe que la carrera ya terminó cuando agitan la **bandera** con cuadros blancos y negros.

You have uncovered the clues. **Have you guessed what I am?**

Ya observaste las pistas. **¿Ya adivinaste qué soy?**

TIRE
LLANTA

STEERING WHEEL
VOLANTE

HEADLIGHT
FARO

ENGINE
MOTOR

NUMBER
NÚMERO

AIR GUN
PISTOLA DE AIRE

FUEL CAN
DEPÓSITO DE COMBUSTIBLE

HARNESS
ARNÉS

HELMET
CASCO

SUIT
TRAJE

TRACK
PISTA

FLAG
BANDERA

If not, here are more clues. Now add them up and you'll see...

1. I am called a stock vehicle. This means that I am a vehicle that could be driven on a public street, but after I am redesigned I can only be driven on a racetrack.

2. I am one of a group of vehicles designed to keep the driver safe while being driven fast. I have a powerful engine, and my strong but light metal tubing frame is covered with thin metal sheeting. A steel tubing cage (called a roll cage) inside me surrounds the driver so he or she will be protected if I roll over or crash.

3. A special seat inside my roll cage wraps around the driver's rib cage. This supports and cushions the driver if I crash.

4. What looks like doors on my sides are really solid panels with cutout windows. The driver climbs into and out of me through one of these openings. After he or she climbs in, the window openings are covered by a mesh made from nylon webbing. This webbing helps keep the driver's arms from coming out of me during a crash.

5. I am 9 feet long, 6 feet wide, and 4$\frac{1}{4}$ feet high (about the same size as an average passenger car).

6. I weigh about 3,400 pounds, about the same weight as three cows.

7. I can go more than 200 miles per hour, but never on a public street or highway. I only go this fast when I'm on a track.

Si no has adivinado, aquí tienes más pistas. Ahora, junta todas las pistas y verás...

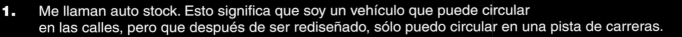

1. Me llaman auto stock. Esto significa que soy un vehículo que puede circular en las calles, pero que después de ser rediseñado, sólo puedo circular en una pista de carreras.

2. Soy parte de un grupo de vehículos diseñados para mantener seguros a los pilotos mientras nos conducen a gran velocidad. Tengo un motor potente y mi chasis de tubos metálicos, ligero pero fuerte, está cubierto con una delgada placa de metal. En mi interior tengo una jaula de tubos de acero que rodea al piloto para protegerlo en caso de volcadura o de choque.

3. Dentro de la jaula hay un asiento especial que rodea el tórax del piloto, para darle soporte y amortiguar los golpes en caso de choque.

4. Lo que parecen puertas a los lados, en realidad son paneles sólidos con aberturas en forma de ventana. El piloto entra y sale a través de una de estas aberturas. Una vez dentro, este espacio se cubre con una malla de nylon. Esta malla impide que los brazos del piloto se salgan del auto en un choque.

5. Mido unos 2.7 metros de largo, 1.82 metros de ancho y 1.30 metros de altura (más o menos el mismo tamaño que un auto de pasajeros promedio).

6. Peso unos 1,500 kilos, casi lo mismo que tres vacas.

7. Puedo ir a más de 320 kilómetros por hora, pero nunca en una calle o en una carretera. Sólo puedo correr así de rápido cuando estoy en una pista.

Do you want to know more about me? Here are some Race Car fun facts.

¿Quieres saber más sobre mí? Aquí tienes unos datos divertidos sobre autos de carreras.

1. The first car to be widely used as a stock car was the Oldsmobile Rocket V-8, which was made in 1949.

2. NASCAR (National Association for Stock Car Auto Racing) is an organization that oversees many types of races across the country. It created a set of rules for stock car racing and a standard size and speed for the cars.

3. The hood, roof, and trunk lid of a stock race car are all standard car parts. The rest of the vehicle is designed and made strictly for racing.

4. A stock race car gets very poor fuel mileage, about 5 to 6 miles per gallon, compared to a street car, which can average between 20 and 50 miles per gallon on a highway.

5. A stock race car holds about 22 gallons of fuel, which is not enough to complete a race. It has to stop and refuel in order to continue racing.

6. Stock race car windshields are made out of Lexan, the same material that is used to make bulletproof glass. This type of glass is very strong and will not shatter and harm the driver if a crash occurs.

1. El primer auto en ser usado comúnmente como auto stock fue el Oldsmobile Rocket V-8, fabricado en 1949.

2. La NASCAR (Asociación Nacional de Carreras de Autos Stock) es una organización que supervisa diversos tipos de carreras en todo el país. Implementó una serie de reglas para las carreras de autos stock, así como el tamaño y la velocidad estándar para dichos vehículos.

3. El cofre, techo y cajuela de un auto stock son partes estándar, mientras que el resto del vehículo se diseña y fabrica específicamente para correr.

4. El combustible de un auto stock de carreras rinde muy poco, entre unos 2.1 y 2.6 kilómetros por litro, comparados con los 8.5 a 21 kilómetros por litro que rinde un auto promedio en carretera.

5. A un auto stock le caben 83 litros, lo cual no es suficiente para una carrera completa. Debe detenerse y cargar gasolina para seguir corriendo.

6. Los parabrisas de los autos stock de carreras están hechos de Lexan, el mismo material que se usa en la fabricación del vidrio a prueba de balas. Este tipo de vidrio es muy fuerte, no se astilla y de esta forma no daña al piloto en caso de accidente.

Who, **What**, Where, When, Why, and How

USE THE QUESTIONS who, what, where, when, why, and how to help the child apply knowledge and process the information in the book. Encourage him or her to investigate, inquire, and imagine.

In the Book...

DO YOU KNOW WHO drives the race car?

DO YOU KNOW WHAT the featured vehicle in the book is?

DO YOU KNOW WHERE the race car is driven?

DO YOU KNOW WHEN the tires on the race car are changed?

DO YOU KNOW WHY the driver wears a harness?

DO YOU KNOW HOW many gallons of fuel the fuel tank holds?

In Your Life...

What protective gear does the race car driver wear that you might wear while playing sports?

CROSS-CURRICULAR EXTENSIONS

Math

There are three race cars: one red, one blue, and one yellow. There are also three race car drivers: Mickey, Peter, and Sam. Mickey drives the blue car and doesn't win; Peter drives the yellow car; Sam finishes behind Mickey.

Which driver finishes in first place? What color car is Sam driving?

Science

Draw and label the parts of a race car.

Social Studies

Do you know which famous NASCAR race is held in Florida each year during the month of February?

Fun Activity

You have uncovered the clues and discovered the race car. Now pretend you are a race car who is trying to find a driver.

ASSIGNMENT
Write an advertisement about yourself as a race car looking for a driver. Draw a picture of yourself to go with the advertisement.

IMAGINE
Who is your first choice for your driver?
What do you look like?
Where are you going to advertise for your driver?
Why do you like or dislike racing?
When do you think you'll stop racing?
How do you plan to win races?

WRITE
Enjoy the writing process while you take what you have imagined and create your advertisement.

Quién, **Qué**, Dónde, Cuándo, Por qué, Cuánto y Cómo

UTILICE LAS PREGUNTAS quién, qué, dónde, cuándo, por qué, cuánto y cómo para ayudar al estudiante a aplicar el conocimiento y procesar la información del libro. Anímelo a investigar, preguntar e imaginar.

En el libro...

¿SABES QUIÉN maneja el auto?

¿SABES QUÉ auto es el que aparece en el libro?

¿SABES EN DÓNDE manejan el auto de carreras?

¿SABES CUÁNDO cambian las llantas del auto de carreras?

¿SABES POR QUÉ el piloto usa un arnés?

¿SABES CUÁNTOS litros de combustible le caben al tanque?

En tu vida...

¿Qué accesorio de protección usan los pilotos de autos de carreras que tú también puedes usar al practicar deportes?

APLICACIÓN EN OTRAS MATERIAS

Matemáticas

Hay tres autos de carreras: uno rojo, uno azul y uno amarillo. También hay tres pilotos: Mickey, Peter y Sam. Mickey maneja el auto azul y no gana; Peter maneja el auto amarillo; Sam termina detrás de Mickey.

¿Qué piloto termina en primer lugar? ¿De qué color es el auto que maneja Sam?

Ciencias

Dibuja y marca las partes de un auto de carreras.

Ciencias sociales

¿Sabes qué famosa carrera de NASCAR se lleva a cabo en Florida cada año, en el mes de febrero?

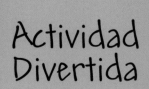

Actividad Divertida

Ya observaste las pistas y descubriste el auto de carreras. Ahora, simula que eres un auto de carreras y estás tratando de encontrar un piloto.

TAREA
Escribe un anuncio en el que te promuevas tú mismo como un auto de carreras en busca de un piloto. Dibuja una imagen de ti mismo para ponerla en el anuncio.

IMAGÍNATE
¿Quién es tu primera elección para ser tu piloto? ¿Cómo te ves?

¿En dónde vas a colocar tu anuncio en busca de un piloto?
¿Por qué sí o por qué no te gustan las carreras?
¿Cuándo crees que vas a dejar de correr?
¿Cómo planeas ganar las carreras?

ESCRIBE
Dedica un momento y disfruta el proceso de narrar por escrito lo que te has imaginado y lo que se te ha ocurrido para tu anuncio.

Judy Zocchi

Judy Zocchi is the creator of the Uncover & Discover series as well as the author of the Global Adventures, Holiday Happenings, Click & Squeak Computer Basics, and Paulie and Sasha series. In addition, she has penned many books under the name of Molly Dingles. Ms. Zocchi is also a lyricist who holds a bachelor's degree in fine arts/theater from Mount Saint Mary's College and a master's degree in educational theater from New York University. She lives in Manasquan, New Jersey.

Russ Daff

Since graduating from Falmouth School of Art in 1993, Russ Daff has enjoyed a varied career. For eight years he worked on numerous projects in the computer games industry, producing titles for Sony PlayStation and PC formats. While designing a wide range of characters and environments for these games, he developed a strong sense of visual impact that he later utilized in his illustration and comic work. Russ now concentrates on his illustration and cartooning full-time. When he is not working, he enjoys painting, writing cartoon stories, and playing bass guitar. He lives in Cambridge, England.